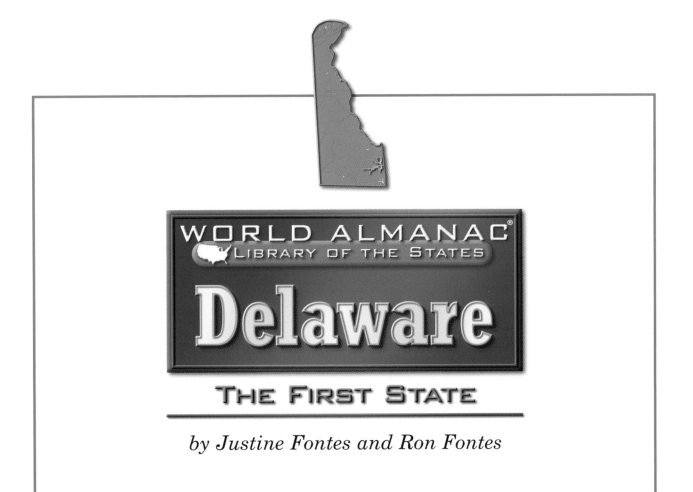

# Delaware

## THE FIRST STATE

*by Justine Fontes and Ron Fontes*

**WORLD ALMANAC® LIBRARY**

**Please visit our web site at: www.worldalmanaclibrary.com**
**For a free color catalog describing World Almanac® Library's list of high-quality books**
**and multimedia programs, call 1-800-848-2928 (USA) or 1-800-387-3178 (Canada).**
**World Almanac® Library's fax: (414) 332-3567.**

Library of Congress Cataloging-in-Publication Data available upon request
from publisher. Fax (414) 336-0157 for the attention of the Publishing
Records Department.

ISBN 0-8368-5148-X (lib. bdg.)
ISBN 0-8368-5319-9 (softcover)

First published in 2003 by
**World Almanac® Library**
330 West Olive Street, Suite 100
Milwaukee, WI 53212 USA

A Creative Media Applications Production
Design: Alan Barnett, Inc.
Copy editor: Laurie Lieb
Fact checker: Joan Verniero
Photo researcher: Jamey O'Quinn
World Almanac® Library project editor: Tim Paulson
World Almanac® Library editors: Mary Dykstra, Gustav Gedatus, Jacqueline Laks Gorman,
  Lyman Lyons
World Almanac® Library art direction: Tammy Gruenewald
World Almanac® Library graphic designers: Scott M. Krall, Melissa Valuch,
  Katherine A. Goedheer

Photo credits: pp. 4-5 © Kevin Fleming/CORBIS; p. 6 (right top) © Robert Pickett/CORBIS;
p. 6 (right bottom) © Royalty-Free/CORBIS; p. 7 (top) © Royalty-Free/CORBIS; p. 7 (bottom)
© AP/Wide World Photos; p. 9 © Hulton Archive/Getty Images; p. 10 © Delaware Office of
Tourism; p. 11 © Hulton Archive/Getty Images; p. 12 © Hulton Archive/Getty Images; p. 13
© Delaware Office of Tourism; p. 14 © Bo Zaunders/CORBIS; p. 15 © Dave G. Houser/CORBIS;
p. 17 © Delaware Office of Tourism; p. 18 © Delaware Office of Tourism; p. 19 © Bob Rowan;
Progressive Image/CORBIS; p. 20 (left) © Kevin Fleming/CORBIS; p. 20 (center) © Delaware
Office of Tourism; p. 20 (right) © Jeffrey L. Rotman/CORBIS; p. 21 (left) © Delaware Office of
Tourism; p. 21 (center) © AP/Wide World Photos; p. 21 (right) © Royalty-Free/CORBIS; p. 23
© Kevin Fleming/CORBIS; p. 26 © Paul A. Souders/CORBIS; p. 27 © AP/Wide World Photos;
p. 29 © Delaware Office of Tourism; p. 31 (top) © AP/Wide World Photos; pp. 31 (bottom), 32
© Delaware Office of Tourism; p. 33 © Kevin Fleming/CORBIS; p. 34 © Delaware Office of
Tourism; p. 35 © Delaware Office of Tourism; p. 36 © Lee Snider; Lee Snider/CORBIS; p. 37 (top)
© Delaware Office of Tourism; p. 37 (bottom) © AP/Wide World Photos; p. 38 © Hulton
Archive/Getty Images; p. 39 (left) © Bettmann/CORBIS; p. 39 (right top) © Bettmann/CORBIS;
p. 39 (right bottom) © Bettmann/CORBIS; p. 40 © Hulton-Deutsch Collection/CORBIS; p. 41
© Bettmann/CORBIS; pp. 42-43 © Hulton Archive/Getty Images; p. 44 (top and bottom)
© Delaware Office of Tourism; p. 45 (top and bottom) © Delaware Office of Tourism

Printed in the United States of America

1 2 3 4 5 6 7 8 9 07 06 05 04 03

# Delaware

# Fair Delaware

Thomas Jefferson was remarking on Delaware's strategic location when he called it a "jewel among the states." The poet John Lofland made a similar comparison, saying Delaware was "like a diamond, diminutive, but having within it inherent value." Indeed, the small state is like a brilliant jewel, reflecting in miniature the great Union to which it belongs.

Delaware played a key role in the Declaration of Independence and the framing of the U.S. Constitution. As the nation grew to be a great industrial power, Delaware's industries grew, too, contributing inventions such as modern milling machinery, affordable record players, and nylon.

Like the United States, Delaware struggles to balance the demands of its industrial north with the very different needs of its southern farms. When the nation was torn apart during the Civil War (1861–1865), Delaware was also divided. Today, Delaware balances old and new, agriculture and high technology, ecology and industry. Delaware has a little bit of everything that makes America great. The Diamond State has a rich mix of cultures: Dutch, Swedish, German, Irish, African American, Native American, and more. The state has good public schools and excellent opportunities for recreation in its beautiful parks and woodlands. Delaware is a haven for all kinds of birds who rest on its shores.

The state is full of historic landmarks and buildings, fascinating museums, and tax-free shopping malls. Delaware has some of the most fabulous mansions ever built, including those by its foremost family, the du Ponts. The state also has a wealth of theater, from Broadway to ballet and from opera to funky blues-rock. Delaware has all that — plus miles and miles of beach.

▶ Map of Delaware showing the interstate highway system, as well as major cities and waterways.

▼ Delaware's beaches attract thousands of visitors each summer.

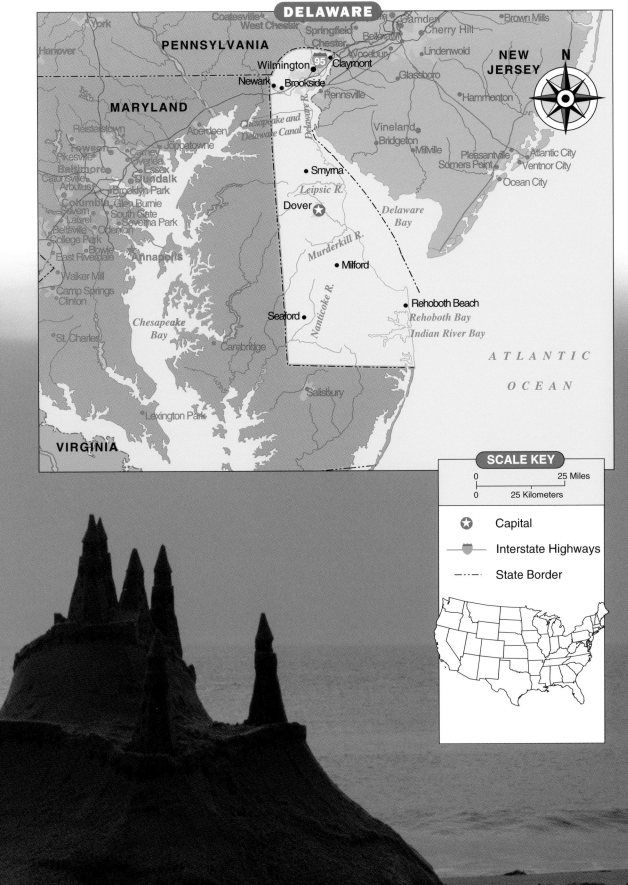

DELAWARE

PENNSYLVANIA

MARYLAND

NEW JERSEY

York
Coatesville
West Chester
Springfield
Chester
Camden
Cherry Hill
Brown Mills
Hanover
Wilmington
Claymont
95
Woodbury
Lindenwold
Newark
Brookside
Pennsville
Glassboro
Reisterstown
Aberdeen
Chesapeake and Delaware Canal
Delaware R.
Vineland
Bridgeton
Hammonton
Towson
Pikesville
Carney
Overlea
Joppatowne
Millville
Pleasantville
Somers Point
Atlantic City
Ventnor City
Baltimore
Essex
Dundalk
Catonsville
Arbutus
Brooklyn Park
Smyrna
Ocean City
Columbia
Glen Burnie
Severn
South Gate
Severna Park
Leipsic R.
Dover
Delaware Bay
Laurel
Beltsville
College Park
Odenton
East Riverdale
Bowie
Annapolis
Murderkill R.
Milford
Walker Mill
Camp Springs
Clinton
Chesapeake Bay
Nanticoke R.
Seaford
Rehoboth Beach
Rehoboth Bay
Indian River Bay
St. Charles
Cambridge
ATLANTIC
OCEAN
Salisbury
VIRGINIA
Lexington Park

SCALE KEY

0          25 Miles
0     25 Kilometers

⭐ Capital

🛡 Interstate Highways

-·-·- State Border

# Fast Facts

DECEMBER 7, 1787

## DELAWARE (DE), The First State, The Diamond State, The Blue Hen State

**Entered Union**

December 7, 1787 (1st state)

| Capital | Population |
| --- | --- |
| Dover | 32,135 |

**Total Population (2000)**

783,600 (45th most populous state). — *Between 1990 and 2000, the state's population increased 17.6 percent.*

| Largest Cities | Population |
| --- | --- |
| Wilmington | 72,664 |
| Dover | 32,135 |
| Newark | 28,547 |
| Milford | 6,732 |
| Seaford | 6,699 |

**Land Area**

1,954 square miles (5,061 square kilometers) (49th largest state)

**State Motto**

"Liberty and Independence"

**State Song**

"Our Delaware," *lyrics by George B. Hynson; music by William M. S. Brow; adopted as the official song by the state legislature in 1925. The first three verses honor each of Delaware's three counties; the fourth verse, written by Donn Devine, praises and pledges loyalty to the state.*

**State Bird**

Blue hen chicken

**State Fish**

Weakfish — *Smart fishermen use a net to scoop up the weakfish they've hooked — the fish are named for the fact that hooks tear easily out of their tender (weak) mouths. Weakfish are also known as sea or gray trout. Like trout, they have long, thin bodies.*

**State Insect**

Ladybug — *The ladybug was adopted as the state insect by Delaware's legislature on April 25, 1974, after a second-grade class from Milford launched a campaign on behalf of the beautiful bug.*

**State Flower**

Peach blossom

**State Tree**

American holly

**State Mineral**

Sillimanite — *This aluminum silicate was named after the American chemist who discovered it.*

**State Colors**

Colonial blue and buff

## PLACES TO VISIT

**Winterthur Museum, Garden, and Library,** *Wilmington*
The country house of Henry Francis du Pont grew to accommodate his amazing antique collection. The brilliant gardens feature rare pine trees and the new Enchanted Woods for children, with delights such as an azalea maze.

**Delaware History Museum,** *Wilmington*
A renovated 1940s Woolworth store houses an interactive multimedia exhibit spanning four hundred years of state history. Visitors can learn while they play in *Grandma's Attic.*

**Trees of the States, Delaware Technical & Community College,** *Georgetown*
Visitors stroll through the only state tree collection complete in a single U.S. location.

For other places and events, see p. 44.

For other places and events, see p. 44.

## BIGGEST, BEST, AND MOST

- Cape Henlopen State Park is home to the highest sand dune between Massachusetts and North Carolina. Great Dune towers 80 feet (24.4 meters) over the coastline.

- Dover Air Force Base houses the biggest plane that the U.S. Air Force flies. The C-5 Galaxy is 247 feet (75 m) long and has a wingspan of nearly 223 feet (68 m).

## STATE FIRSTS

- **1638** Swedish and Finnish colonists in New Sweden built the first log homes in America.

- **1787** Delaware became the first state to ratify the U.S. Constitution and enter the Union. In honor of this, Delaware marches first during all inaugural parades.

- **1937** Wallace Hume Carothers invented the world's first synthetic fiber, nylon, while working in the DuPont company's research department.

## Chick Mix-Up

Ⓞne of Delaware's most important industries started with a mistake. In 1923, Cecile Steele of Sussex County ordered fifty chicks from a farm supplier to provide eggs and meat for her family. Instead, she received five hundred! Steele raised the chicks in an old piano crate and sold some to neighborhood farmers. The state now raises four hundred chickens for every Delawarean and is a leading producer of poultry products. Chickens generate over $500 million for the state each year.

## Little State, Big Business

Ⓐn early immigrant to Delaware founded one of the largest companies in the world. Eleuthère Irénée du Pont came to the United States in 1799 and established the DuPont Corporation on the Brandywine River, near Wilmington. At first, the company made only high-quality gunpowder. Later, DuPont diversified into other products requiring chemical expertise. The company's lab has been the site of important inventions, including nylon, Dacron, Lucite, Teflon, Mylar, neoprene (synthetic rubber), and Corian (a durable material used for kitchen counters and cutting boards). The DuPont Corporation and family have done much to shape the state. DuPont now operates in seventy countries.

# Where North Meets South

As I believe the voice of my constituents and of all sensible and honest men is in favor of independence, my own judgment concurs with them. I vote for independence.
— *Caesar Rodney, July 2, 1776*

Long before any Europeans explored the area, the Lenni Lenape built villages of wigwams, farmed, hunted, and gathered wild foods in the area now known as Delaware. As European settlers started moving in, the tribe (whom the English called the Delaware Indians) moved to Pennsylvania, then Ohio, and finally beyond the Mississippi River. By the 1770s, almost all of Delaware's Native Americans had been forced out. Only a small number of the Nanticoke tribe remain in the southern part of the state.

## First Europeans

The first European to visit Delaware was Henry Hudson, an English sailor hired by the Dutch East India Company, a large import business, to find a water route to the Far East. Hudson sailed into Delaware Bay in 1609. A year later, Captain Samuel Argall was sailing for Virginia's first governor, Baron De La Warr, when his ship was blown off course by a storm. Argall found himself in a strange bay, which he named after his patron.

Delaware's first European settlers came from Hoorn, in the Netherlands, in 1631. Their ship, *De Walvis,* (the *Whale),* landed at Zwaanendael (Swan Valley) near present-day Lewes. A dispute with the local Lenni Lenape chief ended with the settlement being wiped out.

In 1638, a group of Swedes built Fort Christina, Delaware's first permanent white settlement, near what is now Wilmington. Many Finns were among the early settlers of the colony known as "New Sweden." The Finns and Swedes built the first log houses in America. The colony earned money by exporting tobacco and furs.

The Dutch resented the Swedish claim to the area,

### Native Americans of Delaware

Lenni Lenape (also known as Delaware)

Nanticoke

### DID YOU KNOW?

The captain of the *Kalmar Nyckel,* the Swedish ship that brought settlers to Delaware's New Sweden colony, was Peter Minuit. His previous experience included buying the island of Manhattan from local Native tribes while he was director-general of New Netherland. Manhattan is now part of present-day New York City.

and in 1651, they built Fort Casimer as a stronghold from which to watch their rivals. In 1654, the Swedes captured the fort. Then a year later, the Dutch reclaimed Fort Casimer and captured Fort Christina.

Delaware passed into British possession in 1664, along with the Dutch colony of New Netherland, renamed New York. In 1673, the Dutch recaptured the region, but a year later, they gave it back to England without bloodshed. Why all the fuss over this small patch of territory? In the age of sea travel, Delaware's location made it a vital strategic location. The state is one long, natural harbor to the east, facing the Atlantic Ocean, and it also has access to the Chesapeake Bay, another large, natural harbor. The Delaware River offers a navigable route inland.

In 1682, William Penn founded the Pennsylvania colony and gained Delaware for access to the ocean. Penn and Lord Baltimore, of the Maryland colony, argued over borders. Meanwhile, the people living in Delaware felt they were underrepresented in Pennsylvania's legislature, and petitioned for the right to form their own government. In 1704, Penn agreed to let the "Three Lower Counties," as Delaware was known, have their own assembly.

Thanks to its location, by the 1730s, Delaware was already becoming a vital grain port. A shipbuilding center grew up where the Christina and Delaware Rivers meet.

▼ English Quaker William Penn negotiates a treaty with the Delaware Leni Lenape leaders.

The rivers gave ships access to mills. The area became one of America's busiest manufacturing districts.

In 1774, the Three Lower Counties sent delegates to the First Continental Congress in Philadelphia. A year later, Delaware's borders were declared, but the area was ruled by the governor of Pennsylvania until the Revolutionary War (1775–1783).

## Independence

In 1775, Delaware's Continental Regiment assembled at Dover Green before marching off to join General George Washington. Delaware sent almost 4,000 soldiers to fight in the Revolutionary War, and they were among the best.

In 1776, the American colonists drafted a document that would help define the purpose of the war: the Declaration of Independence. The Second Continental Congress met in the colonial capital of Philadelphia to debate the document that would turn the colonies into a free and independent nation. Delaware played a key role. When the Continental Congress was ready for the crucial vote, one of Delaware's three delegates was home sick in Dover. When he heard his vote was needed to break the tie between Delaware's other two delegates, Caesar Rodney rode 86 miles (138 km) to

▼ Woodburn has been the official governor's mansion since 1965. Built in 1790, this Dover mansion was once a station on the Underground Railroad.

Philadelphia, through a stormy night, to cast the deciding vote in favor of independence. The Declaration was officially adopted the following day, July 4, 1776.

When the war was finally over in 1783, the newly free nation was faced with the task of developing its own government. Many months were spent debating the form that government should take: How would the nation's leaders be chosen? What powers would they have? How would those powers be held in check?

The Constitution was rewritten many times in an attempt to define a government that would improve on the old system of King and Parliament. The document would not take effect until representatives from nine out of thirteen states ratified, or approved, it. Delaware's delegates were the first to do so. On December 7, 1787, Delaware became the first state to ratify the Constitution, and with that vote, they became the first official state in the new Union. The Constitution was ratified in the Golden Fleece Tavern, about a block from what is now Dover's Constitution Park.

## Work and War

In 1802, Eleuthère Irénée du Pont built a gunpowder mill on the Brandywine River, near Wilmington. In 1812, when England tried to take back its former colonies, du Pont's business boomed. During the War of 1812 (1812–1815), British ships patrolled Delaware Bay, raided the shores of the Chesapeake, and shelled the port at Lewes. Lacking their own ammunition, the defenders of Lewes gathered up British cannonballs and fired them back until the British fled to the Bermudas. This kind of resourcefulness and determination proved to the British that the United States would stay free.

During the mid-nineteenth century, Delaware's industries continued to grow. Shipyards, foundries, machine shops, and textile mills sprang up in the north of the state. Thanks to abundant

# John Dickinson

Philadelphia lawyer John Dickinson was elected to Pennsylvania's legislature in 1762. At the Stamp Act Congress of 1765, Dickinson expressed his opposition to British taxes in a declaration of rights and grievances. His widely read *Letters From a Farmer in Pennsylvania to the Inhabitants of the British Colonies* (1768) called for colonial rights. Dickinson had hoped the colonies could reconcile with England, but after the Battle of Lexington, he joined the Revolutionary War. He represented Delaware at the Constitutional Convention in 1787. Dickinson played an important role in drafting the U.S. Constitution, and his influence helped Delaware and Pennsylvania become the first states to ratify it. For this and his earlier patriotic writings, Dickinson is known as the "Penman of the Revolution."

waterpower, Wilmington became an industrial center. Better roads, plus the opening of the Chesapeake and Delaware Canal in 1829 and the completion of the Philadelphia, Wilmington, and Baltimore Railroad in 1856, made the shipping of goods and supplies cheaper, faster, and easier.

Although businesses were successful, the state struggled to find affordable labor for its farms and factories. One solution was to use "indentured servants." The system of getting poor people to sign contracts binding them to work for a certain number of years was started in England in the sixteenth century. In colonial times, employers would pay a servant's passage from Scotland, Ireland, or England to America. There the servant would work for food and shelter — but no salary — until his or her contract was completed. If ill-treated, and they often were, indentured servants could not complain or quit. They had no more rights than slaves — only the promise of freedom and farmland at the end of their contracts. Even that, however, was not assured. Often employers cheated indentured servants out of their land by claiming that the servants were lazy or had tried to run away. Many indentured servants worked thirty to forty years with broken promises and exhaustion as their only rewards.

▼ In 1860, Delaware had fewer than two thousand slaves and twenty thousand free African Americans. The Thirteenth Amendment to the Constitution abolished slavery throughout the United States in 1865.

The other solution to Delaware's labor shortage was slavery, but many opposed the sale, ownership, and use of human beings as slaves. In the early nineteenth century, the state passed laws forbidding the bringing in of new slaves. However, slaves continued to work in Delaware's southern farmlands until the end of the Civil War and the passing of the Thirteenth Amendment in 1865, abolishing slavery.

Delaware was divided on the question of slavery. Many of the state's Quakers and Methodists wanted to abolish slavery in Delaware, but many other Delawareans sympathized with the Confederate cause. Most of the state supported the Union, and although they were never completely trusted by the rest of the North, many Delawareans fought in the Union Army. DuPont's factory profited greatly during the bloody, four-year Civil War, supplying both sides with gunpowder.

▲ The Tubman-Garrett Riverfront Park honors Wilmington's two most famous Underground Railroad "conductors," Harriet Tubman and Thomas Garrett.

## The Railroad to Freedom

One way the abolitionists (people opposed to slavery) took action was by helping slaves escape. The Underground Railroad was a network of people who sheltered slaves on their way to the North. Because of its location, Delaware was one of the last stops on the road to freedom.

One of the most famous "conductors" of the Underground Railroad was a Quaker named Thomas Garrett. Quakers are committed to peace, and they declared their opposition to slavery as early as 1688. Garrett grew up deeply believing in the principle of equality, as stated in the Declaration of Independence. The issue of slavery came home to him in 1813, when a free black woman working in Garrett's home was kidnapped to be sold into slavery. Garrett found the kidnappers and brought the woman safely home. From then on, he dedicated himself to the struggle to free all slaves.

When he lived in Wilmington, Garrett became friends with leading abolitionists, including former Maryland slave Harriet Tubman. During the decades before the Civil War, Garrett, Tubman, and others helped slaves escape safely through Delaware to Pennsylvania at the risk of arrest.

### Useful Canal

The Chesapeake and Delaware Canal was dug by twenty-six hundred men using picks and shovels for five years, from 1824 to 1829. (The men earned an average of seventy-five cents a day.) The canal, which is 14 miles (22.5 km) long, 450 feet (137 m) wide, and 35 feet (10.7 m) deep, connects the Delaware River and the Chesapeake Bay, trimming nearly 300 miles (483 km) off the journey ships must travel between Delaware and Baltimore.

A hardworking and successful blacksmith, Garrett lost everything he owned in 1848 to pay a $5,400 fine when he was found guilty of helping runaway slaves. The judge at his trial told Garrett, "I hope you will never be caught at this business again." Garrett replied, "Friend, I haven't a dollar in the world, but if thee knows a fugitive who needs a breakfast, send him to me."

In 1860, the Maryland State Legislature offered a $10,000 reward for anyone able to arrest Garrett for slave stealing. Garrett continued to do all he could to end slavery. Garrett personally helped some 2,700 slaves reach freedom. When the Fifteenth Amendment to the U.S. Constitution — giving former slaves the right to vote — became law on March 30, 1870, Wilmington's African Americans celebrated by carrying the eighty-one-year-old Garrett on their shoulders through the streets. They called him "Our Moses." Garrett died the following year.

## Peace, Prosperity, and Prejudice

After the Civil War, poll taxes (special fees for voting) prevented most of Delaware's African Americans from voting. Then in 1897, poll taxes were replaced by a literacy test that also effectively eliminated the black vote, because few African Americans at the time could read. This situation was reversed in 1901, when Delaware ratified the Fifteenth Amendment to the U.S. Constitution, granting African Americans in the state the right to vote.

After the turmoil of the Civil War had ended, Delaware enjoyed many decades of peace and prosperity. In the 1870s, rich peach growers built huge mansions, many of which are still standing today. When a virus called peach yellows destroyed the trees, Delaware's farmers grew other crops, and the state's industries continued to expand.

During World War I (1917–1918), the small state did its part, sending 10,000 soldiers to fight overseas. In the 1920s, Delaware's chicken industry got its start. Then, like the rest of the world, Delaware suffered through the Great Depression of the 1930s. Changes to the state government

▲ The original Delaware Memorial Bridge opened on August 16, 1951. It was an immediate success. Due to increased leisure and commercial traffic, a second span opened in 1968. The double-span bridge provides an important link in the corridor from Boston, Massachusetts, to Washington, D.C.

## DID YOU KNOW?

The Underground Railroad was not a train, but a network of places where runaway slaves could find shelter. "Conductors" were people who risked their own lives to harbor escaped slaves and guide them to the next "stop" on their dangerous journey north to freedom.

helped poor people find employment. Relief also came from the federal government, with programs such as the Works Progress Administration, which hired unemployed people to build parks and other public facilities.

Along with the rest of the United States, Delaware recovered economically during the industrial boom of World War II (1941–1945). Delaware's mills and factories turned out war materials. Dravo Shipyards became the state's top employer, going from four hundred workers in 1940 to eleven thousand at the height of the war. Dover Air Force Base was the site of secret rocket development.

After the war, Delaware's industries continued to grow. The building of the Delaware Memorial Bridge in 1951 linked the state to New Jersey, making transportation to big markets in that state and beyond even easier.

Unfortunately, not every sector of the population was sharing in the state's profits. In 1967 and again in 1968, unemployed blacks rioted in Wilmington. The National Guard was called in to restore order. A fair-housing law was then passed, making it illegal to deny people a home based on their race. African Americans presently constitute about 20 percent of Delaware's total population. Some of these residents still face daily challenges as the state strives for change in the twenty-first century.

## Malls and Main Street

**M**any towns across the United States are losing business to sprawling malls. Main Street stores close and downtowns become ghost towns. To prevent this, Delaware's Economic Development Office launched its Main Street Program in 1994 to encourage historic preservation and landscaping, as well as help towns attract business. Delaware City, Dover, Seaford, Smyrna, Rehoboth Beach, Greater Brandywine Village, Middletown, and Newark are all Delaware Main Street communities.

*Below:* Patrons stroll down a quaint main street in Chester. The Tudor-style buildings and mom-and-pop shops attract shoppers to the commercial district. The Main Street Program works to preserve historic buildings such as these for shops, museums, and offices.

# North and South Together

> Cultivate peace and harmony with all . . .
> —*George Washington's Farewell Address,*
> *September 17, 1796*

Delaware is densely populated and growing. The growth of industries such as synthetic fabric and poultry production drew immigrants in the 1920s, and the state enjoyed another growth spurt after World War II. In 2000, the state's average population density was about 401 people per square mile (155 per sq km). Roughly three-quarters of Delaware's people live in urban areas. Much of the state's population is concentrated in the northern half, specifically in the Wilmington-Newark metropolitan area. Rapid development is resulting in increased urban crowding.

Delaware is divided into a mostly urban, industrialized north and a small-town, agricultural south. However, all its citizens are proud to live together in the peaceful state of Delaware.

### Age Distribution in Delaware
(2000 Census)

| | |
|---|---|
| 0–4 | 51,531 |
| 5–19 | 166,719 |
| 20–24 | 51,665 |
| 25–44 | 236,441 |
| 45–64 | 175,518 |
| 65 & over | 101,726 |

### Patterns of Immigration

The total number of people who immigrated to Delaware in 1998 was 1,063. Of that number, the largest immigrant groups were from India (13.3%), Mexico (12.7%), and the People's Republic of China (7.4%)

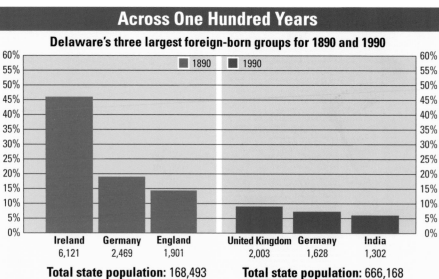

**Across One Hundred Years**

Delaware's three largest foreign-born groups for 1890 and 1990

■ 1890  ■ 1990

| Ireland 6,121 | Germany 2,469 | England 1,901 | United Kingdom 2,003 | Germany 1,628 | India 1,302 |

**Total state population: 168,493**
**Total foreign-born: 13,161 (7.8%)**

**Total state population: 666,168**
**Total foreign-born: 22,275 (3.3%)**

## Ethnicities

About five hundred members of the Nanticoke tribe still live in southwestern Delaware. The Nanticoke were known as People of the Tide Water. They lived in wigwams made of wooden poles covered with skins, bark, or mats of rushes. The first European settlers to move to the state came from the Netherlands, Sweden, and England. Later, immigrants came from France, Germany, Italy, Greece, Ireland, Scotland, and Poland. Asians and Hispanics are the fastest-growing groups today. However, most Delawareans, about 93 percent, were born in the United States. African Americans make up about half the population of Delaware's largest city, Wilmington.

▲ Visitors to Wilmington's Little Italy enjoy fine Italian pastries and treats.

## Religion

Methodists and Roman Catholics are the leading religious groups in Delaware. Over 26 percent of the population belongs to each of these forms of Christianity. Delaware is also home to Presbyterians, Episcopalians, and other religious groups.

About two hundred Amish families live on farms to the west of Dover. The Amish are a strict sect, or religious denomination, of the Mennonites. The Mennonite faith

**DID YOU KNOW?**

Wilmington's Holy Trinity Episcopal Church is believed to be the oldest active Protestant church in North America. Known as Old Swedes, the church was built in 1698; stained glass windows were added in the late 1800s.

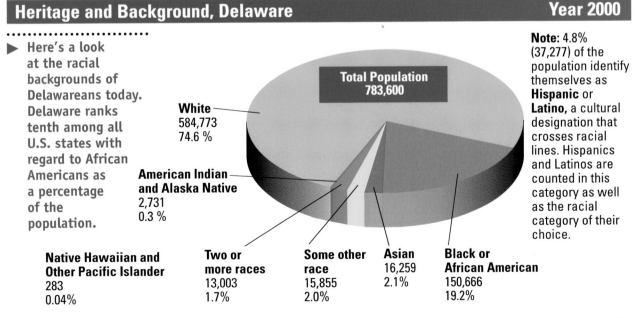

## Heritage and Background, Delaware — Year 2000

▶ Here's a look at the racial backgrounds of Delawareans today. Delaware ranks tenth among all U.S. states with regard to African Americans as a percentage of the population.

**Total Population 783,600**

**Note:** 4.8% (37,277) of the population identify themselves as **Hispanic** or **Latino,** a cultural designation that crosses racial lines. Hispanics and Latinos are counted in this category as well as the racial category of their choice.

White
584,773
74.6 %

American Indian and Alaska Native
2,731
0.3 %

Native Hawaiian and Other Pacific Islander
283
0.04%

Two or more races
13,003
1.7%

Some other race
15,855
2.0%

Asian
16,259
2.1%

Black or African American
150,666
19.2%

was founded by Menno Simons in Germany in the sixteenth century. Both Mennonites and their stricter cousins, the Amish, reject military service and all forms of violence. They prefer to live close to the land, with a minimum of modern conveniences. Mennonites use electricity and automobiles, but the Amish continue to use candles and horse-drawn carriages. Both groups are famous for their excellent produce, preserves, baked goods, and handicrafts.

Quakers played a key role in Delaware's past as "conductors" on the Underground Railroad, which helped slaves escape from the South. Like the Mennonites and Amish, Quakers are committed to nonviolence.

| Educational Levels of Delaware Workers (age 25 and over) | |
|---|---|
| Less than 9th grade | 25,490 |
| 9th to 12th grade, no diploma | 64,046 |
| High school graduate, including equivalency | 161,760 |
| Some college, no degree or associate degree | 134,445 |
| Bachelor's degree | 80,376 |
| Graduate or professional degree | 48,541 |

▼ The skyline of Wilmington, Delaware's largest city. It is often referred to as "the corporate capital of the world."

## Education

The Delaware state legislature created a public education fund in 1796, but the public school system did not get underway until 1829. Funding and teaching were not always adequate, and African Americans were not allowed to attend the public schools. Some blacks were able to get an education at Quaker schools.

School attendance became required by Delaware law in 1907. The early twentieth century was a time of big improvements in the state's school system. Industrialist and philanthropist Pierre S. du Pont contributed several million dollars to Delaware's school system.

The state's schools were desegregated in 1954 in response to a Supreme Court decision. However, until 1978, most African Americans were still attending predominantly black schools in Wilmington, while whites went to school in the suburbs. Court-ordered busing helped make integration a reality for Delaware's public school students.

Delaware's first institution of higher education, the University of Delaware at Newark, began as a private academy in 1743. The state has about ten degree-granting institutions, including Dover's Delaware State University (established in 1891) and Wesley College (1873).

The University of Delaware is a cultural center for the state. The University Gallery offers exhibits of local and national art and artifacts and serves as a teaching museum for students interested in pursuing careers as museum curators or in the fields of art, art history, or archaeology.

The university also has an internationally renowned collection of mineral specimens from around the world in its Mineralogical Museum, as well as a Center for Black Culture that presents performances to promote cultural and ethnic awareness.

### The Delaware Tribe

Before European settlers came, Delaware was occupied by the Lenni Lenape tribe, also known as the Delaware. This sedentary tribe supplemented the farming of corn, beans, and squashes by hunting and gathering food from the wild. The Delaware made wampum belts to record special events and as ceremonial gifts. Wampum beads are carved from shells, then strung together in symbolic designs. The Delaware were part of the Algonquian language group.

# Small but Perfect

> Mr. President, the gentleman who has just spoken represents
> a state which has two counties when the tide is up
> — and only three when it is down.
>
> — *John J. Ingalls, U.S. senator from Kansas from 1873 to 1891,*
> *responding to a Delaware senator*

The only state smaller than Delaware is Rhode Island. Delaware is shaped like a steep triangle, with the Delaware River, Delaware Bay, and the Atlantic Ocean on its eastern side, Maryland to the south and west, and Pennsylvania to the north. At its longest, from north to south, Delaware is only about 96 miles (154 km). At its widest, from east to west, the state is only about 36 miles (58 km). Yet Delaware has a sampling of almost all the things that make the United States great: rolling rivers, beautiful beaches, rich farmland, wildlife, and woods.

**Highest Point**

**Ebright Road in New Castle County**
448 feet (137 m) above sea level

## Part of a Peninsula

About 95 percent of Delaware is on a peninsula, a piece of land surrounded on three sides by water. The "Delmarva Peninsula" includes Delaware and parts of two other states, Maryland and Virginia.

Delaware is one of the flattest of the fifty states, full of level farmlands, gentle hills, and grassy lawns. Delaware is also the lowest state in the country, with an average elevation of only 60 feet (18 m) above sea level. Some 381

▼ *From left to right: Rehoboth Beach; Trussom Pond; horseshoe crab at Cape Henlopen; Hoopes Reservoir; Fourteen Foot Bank Lighthouse, Delaware Bay; dolphins swimming*

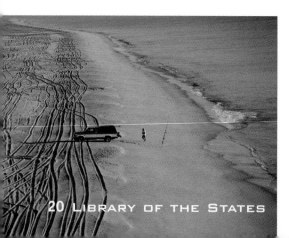

miles (613 km) of it sink below the sea at high tide. The highest part of Delaware is a small area of rolling hills in the extreme north, part of the Piedmont Plateau. The rest of the state is part of the Atlantic coastal plain, which stretches from New Jersey to Florida. It consists of low, gentle hills sloping down to the sea.

### Three Counties

Delaware is divided into three counties: New Castle in the north, Kent in the middle, and Sussex in the south. Sussex County has the richest soil and the longest growing season, but the other two counties also have fine farmland. Sussex is also home to the 30,000-acre (12,141-ha) Great Cypress Swamp, the country's northernmost cypress swamp.

### Rivers and Lakes

There are no large rivers inside Delaware. However, the state's northeastern boundary is the lower Delaware River and its estuary, Delaware Bay. (An estuary is the wide, tidal mouth of a river.) Delaware has no large lakes, but it has many small bodies of water for swimming and fishing. Delaware Bay and the Delaware River are deep enough to allow oceangoing craft as far north as Wilmington. The remainder of the state's rivers are too shallow for anything except small boats. The Chesapeake and Delaware Canal cuts across the upper part of the state linking the Delaware River with Chesapeake Bay.

### Climate

Delaware's climate is humid and temperate. Because the entire state is small, low, and flat, there is little difference in the mild weather across the state. Ocean breezes and warm currents make temperatures along the Atlantic Coast comfortably cooler in summer and a bit warmer in winter

**Average January temperature**
Wilmington: 32°F (0°C)

**Average July temperature**
Wilmington: 80°F (26.6°C)

**Average yearly rainfall**
Wilmington: 40 inches (102 cm)

**Average yearly snowfall**
Wilmington: 20 inches (51 cm)

**DID YOU KNOW?**

One of the bald cypress trees in Great Cypress Swamp may be Delaware's oldest tree. About six hundred years old, the Patriarch Tree is 50 feet (15 m) across.

**Largest Lakes**

There are no large natural lakes, but dams have created reservoirs.

**Hoopes Reservoir**
192 acres (78 hectares)

**Lums Pond**
189 acres (76 ha)

**Noxontown Pond**
159 acres (64 ha)

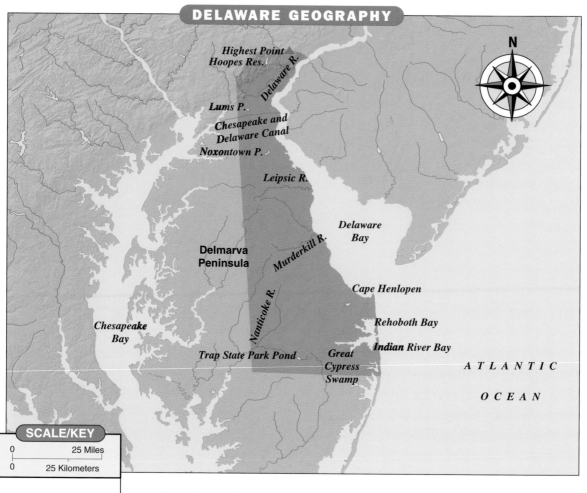

**SCALE/KEY**

0        25 Miles

0        25 Kilometers

▲ Highest Point

than inland areas. Inland Delaware tends to get humid in the summer. Although Delaware is in the storm track for disturbances from both the Gulf of Mexico and the continental weather system from the west, the state's placement between the Atlantic Ocean in the east and Chesapeake Bay in the west eases the effect of these storms.

## Plants and Animals

A little less than one-third of Delaware is covered in woodlands that support a wide variety of trees: beeches, dogwoods, maples, pines, and others. Azaleas, blueberries, cranberries, crocuses, hibiscus, honeysuckle, lady's slippers, violets, and water lilies are among the many flowers that thrive in Delaware. Cattails and cordgrass grow in the state's salt marshes.

Deer are the largest animals in Delaware. White-tailed deer and small game, such as raccoon, opossum, red and gray foxes, rabbit, and muskrat, are found throughout the state.

Delaware lies within the Atlantic migratory flyway, the

path migrating birds travel each year to reach warm southern climates before winter and to return north in the spring. Bombay Hook National Wildlife Refuge in Kent County offers the best bird-watching in the Middle Atlantic region. The marshy shore of the Delaware Bay is a refuge for local birds and travelers, too, including Canada geese, snow geese, hawks, bobwhite quail, and red-winged blackbirds. Delaware supports a variety of ducks, as well as many shorebirds such as egrets and herons.

The ribbed mussels, fiddler crabs, clams, oysters, and eels that thrive in the state's salt marshes are favorite foods for many birds. Shorebirds also love to feast on the horseshoe crab eggs laid on Delaware's beaches each spring.

Many different varieties of fish swim in Delaware's rivers and ponds, including bass, bluegill, catfish, perch, shad, trout, and weakfish. Off the coast, sea bass, sea trout, and bluefish are found. The state's reptiles include snapping turtles and diamondback terrapins. The bog turtle, bald eagle, and piping plover are among the state's threatened animals.

**Major Rivers**

**Nanticoke River**
436 miles (702 km)

**Murderkill River**
65 miles (105 km)

**Leipsic River**
38 miles (61 km)

▼ This flock of birds is traveling the Atlantic flyway, the migratory path that passes over Delaware Bay. The Bay is a great place for bird-watching during both the spring and fall migrations.

# Chickens and Corporations

> We all know each other, and if there's a problem,
> we can bring the people and resources together
> to solve it. That is why I say Delaware
> is small enough to work.
>
> — *Pierre S. du Pont, Delaware's governor from 1976 to 1984*

Delaware's economy has grown with the nation's, from farming and sea trade to manufacturing, and, most recently, financial services. The state's economy began with abundant crops of wheat and corn. Lumber was harvested to build homes and ships. Oliver Evans's innovations in milling technology led to an unprecedented success in processing local wheat into flour, which could be shipped to foreign markets through the port in nearby Philadelphia. Iron manufacturing provided profits for many years. Iron shipbuilding was centered in Wilmington, where the first iron-hulled, propeller-driven steamship, the *Bangor*, was launched in 1844. All of the steel for the entire suspended superstructure of the Brooklyn Bridge was manufactured in Wilmington.

Delaware is small but rich. Thanks to good education and state incentives for businesses, Delaware's workers enjoy some of the highest salaries in the United States.

## Agriculture, Forestry, Fishing, and Mining

Delaware's two southern counties are full of small farms. The state contains about twenty-six hundred farms, with an average size of 223 acres (90 ha). Delaware's most important farm product is broiler chickens. Broilers are young chickens raised for broiling or roasting, as opposed to those raised for frying (fryers). The state's vast fields of soybeans and corn are mostly used as chicken feed.

Other important farm products are greenhouse and nursery products, as well as various fruits and vegetables. Peaches used to be a key crop, which is why the state flower

| Top Employers (of workers age sixteen and over) |
|---|
| Services ...... 40.6% |
| Wholesale and retail trade ....14.4% |
| Manufacturing ..13.2% |
| Finance, insurance, and real estate ..11.6% |
| Construction .... 7.4% |
| Transportation, communications, and public utilities ........ 6.7% |
| Federal, state, and local government (including military) ....... 5.2% |
| Agriculture, forestry, fisheries, and mining ..... 1.1% |

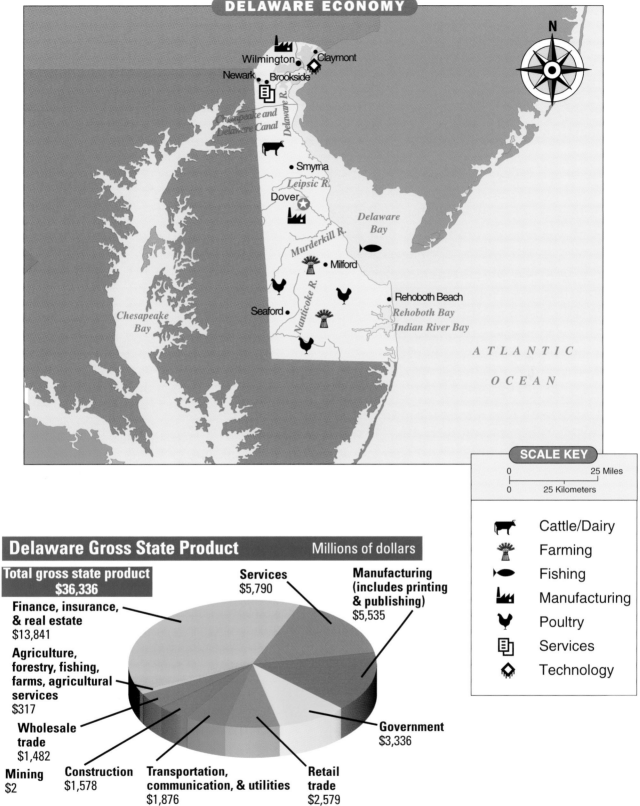

## SCALE KEY

0            25 Miles

0            25 Kilometers

- Cattle/Dairy
- Farming
- Fishing
- Manufacturing
- Poultry
- Services
- Technology

## Delaware Gross State Product — Millions of dollars

**Total gross state product $36,336**

Services $5,790

Manufacturing (includes printing & publishing) $5,535

Finance, insurance, & real estate $13,841

Agriculture, forestry, fishing, farms, agricultural services $317

Wholesale trade $1,482

Mining $2

Construction $1,578

Transportation, communication, & utilities $1,876

Retail trade $2,579

Government $3,336

is the peach blossom. The Spanish brought peach trees to Delaware in the 1500s. By the 1600s, peaches were so abundant they were fed to the pigs. By 1875, six million baskets were being shipped by sail and steamboat. However, in the 1890s, a virus known as peach yellows killed the trees, and farmers were forced to switch to other crops, such as apples, strawberries, and melons.

Woodlots are scattered throughout Delaware's farmland. The harvesting of pines, oaks, and sweet gums is practiced on a small scale. Fishing is also a small industry. Delaware crabs are a great delicacy. The catch also includes oysters, clams, and sea trout.

Delaware's small mining industry depends mostly on the production of sand, granite, gravel, and clay, which are used to make bricks and tiles. Magnesium compounds extracted from seawater are used to make chemical products and medicines.

## Manufacturing

Delaware has an exciting history as a center for industry and invention. In the late 1700s and early 1800s, the state had a thriving shipbuilding industry. In 1785, Oliver Evans invented new flour-milling machinery that paved the way for modern factories. The DuPont Corporation supplied gunpowder for the War of 1812 and the Civil War. In 1907, DuPont was sued under the Sherman Anti-Trust Act for having a monopoly on gunpowder. The company switched its focus and began manufacturing chemicals. In 1931, it began development of a synthetic (human-made) substitute for silk, especially for women's stockings.

In 1937, a DuPont researcher named Wallace Carothers created the first strands of a strong fiber called nylon, which was introduced to the public at the 1938 New York World's Fair. Nylon freed the U.S. from depending on Japan for silk. During World War II, nylon became a popular

▲ The Chesapeake and Delaware Canal is one of two commercially viable sea-level waterways in the United States today.

### Corporate Capital of the World

In 1981, Delaware's governor, Pierre S. du Pont, signed the Financial Center Development Act. This law removed limits on interest charges. Credit card companies and banks profit by charging interest on the loans. The state also gives big banks a tax break: The more money a bank earns, the less tax it pays. Banks scrambled to set up offices in the state. Delaware has low taxes for corporations and allows businesses to incorporate in Delaware even if they do business elsewhere. As a result, over half the country's five hundred leading industrial corporations are incorporated in the tiny state of Delaware. The state also favors international finance and insurance companies.

substitute for silk among the Allied nations (those at war against Japan, Germany, and Italy). Nylon was used to make parachutes, tires, flak jackets, and other materials the Allies needed during the war — as well as stockings.

Other important state industries include motor vehicles and parts, precision instruments, plastic and rubber goods, leather goods, paper products, printing and publishing, textiles, and food processing (canning).

## Transportation, Services, and Tourism

Delaware's location has always been a tremendous economic advantage. Thanks to Delaware Bay and the state's many rivers, Delaware is a natural shipping hub. The digging of the Chesapeake and Delaware Canal opened a waterway between the Delaware River and the Chesapeake Bay in 1829.

By land, Delaware has easy access to Philadelphia, Baltimore, and Washington, D.C. The state has about 5,780 miles (9,300 km) of public roads, including major highways linking the urban north with the coast and the agricultural south. Shortly after the Canal was completed, railroads came to Delaware. Today, the state has about 230 miles (370 km) of tracks. Amtrak passenger service includes the Metroliner, which stops in Wilmington fifteen times a day and travels at 125 miles (201 km) per hour between New York City and Washington, D.C. Delaware has twenty-three small airports and eleven heliports, but most passengers travel through the Philadelphia International Airport.

Tourism is a major industry. Competing with New Jersey's Atlantic City, the state now offers casino gambling at horse-racing tracks. The state takes 30 percent of the tracks' profits. In addition to its many beaches, Delaware has fourteen state parks, including several that are sanctuaries for birds — and bird-watchers. Tourism has helped raise Delaware's environmental awareness. In 1971, the state passed the Coastal Zone Act to protect the coastal wetlands from real estate development, which would have destroyed vital habitats.

▲ Delaware also attracts tourists because they can shop without paying sales tax. Many stores have factory outlets at the state's popular Rehoboth Beach resort.

### Made in Delaware

**Leading farm products and crops**
Broiler chickens
Soybeans
Corn
Greenhouse and
  nursery products
Eggs

**Other products**
Chemicals
Processed food
Plastics and
  rubber products

# Freedom First

Liberty and Independence,
We will guard with loyal care,
And hold fast to freedom's presence,
In our home state Delaware.

— *Donn Devine's final verse for*
*"Our Delaware,"* Delaware's state song

T wo days after every general election, Delawareans celebrate Return Day in Georgetown with fun, food, speeches, and a ceremonial reading of the election returns. Before mass communications such as television, radio, and daily newspapers, people had to travel to the county seat to find out who had won an election. Return Day continues this tradition of celebrating the election — no matter who won. Winning and losing candidates ride together in a parade of horse-drawn carriages and floats. Democrats and Republicans enjoy food and dancing. It seems fitting that the first state to approve the U.S. Constitution celebrates voting — the freedom to choose leaders — as the most important part of being American.

## The Executive Branch

Like the federal government, Delaware's state government is divided into three parts: the executive branch, the legislative branch, and the judicial branch. The executive branch is led by the governor. The governor appoints many key state officials, including the secretary of state and the secretaries of Delaware's Departments of Education, Labor, and Agriculture. The governor also appoints the members of the Public Service Commission.

If for any reason the governor cannot fulfill his or her duties, the lieutenant governor takes over until the next election. Other elected posts in the executive branch include the attorney general, who is the state's chief legal officer; the treasurer, who oversees the receiving and spending of public money; the auditor of accounts, who makes official

### State Constitution

"... **A**ll men have by nature the rights of worshiping and serving their Creator according to the dictates of their consciences, of enjoying and defending life and liberty ... and in general of obtaining objects suitable to their condition, without injury by one to another; and as these rights are essential to their welfare, for due exercise thereof, power is inherent in them; and therefore all just authority in the institutions of political society is derived from the people, and established with their consent, to advance their happiness; and they may for this end, as circumstances require, from time to time, alter their Constitution of government."

— *Preamble to the 1897 Delaware State Constitution*

| Elected Posts in the Executive Branch | | |
|---|---|---|
| Office | Length of Term | Term Limits |
| Governor | 4 years | 2 terms |
| Lieutenant Governor | 4 years | none |
| Insurance Commissioner | 4 years | none |
| Attorney General | 4 years | none |
| Auditor | 4 years | none |
| Treasurer | 4 years | none |

examinations into state funds; and the insurance commissioner, who regulates the state's insurance industry. Insurance companies sell policies, which are contracts promising to compensate companies or people for various kinds of loss, damage, and disaster.

## The Legislative Branch

The word legislative comes from the Latin words for "law" and "proposing" or "bringing." The legislative branch of Delaware's government makes new laws and changes the state's existing laws. Delaware's legislative branch, which is called the general assembly, consists of a senate and a house of representatives. The people elect twenty-one senators for four-year terms. The house contains forty-one members, also elected directly by Delaware's citizens. Terms in the house last only two years.

▼ The State House in Dover, Delaware's capital city, is topped by a two-hundred-year-old cupola. A cupola is a rounded dome that forms a roof or ceiling.

## The Judicial Branch

This part of the state government is concerned with all of Delaware's courts: the supreme court, the major trial courts, and courts with limited jurisdiction, including family court, the court of common pleas, the justice of the peace court, and the alderman's courts. The supreme court is the state's most powerful court. A judge who sits on a supreme court is called a justice. Delaware's supreme court has five justices (one chief justice and four associate justices). The governor, with the approval of the Senate, appoints them. Justices can serve an unlimited number of twelve-year terms.

Delaware's major trial courts are the court of chancery and the superior court. The court of chancery rules over land sales, estates (wills and inheritances), and business disputes. The superior court judges important criminal trials. The court of common pleas is the court that hears cases concerning minor offenses or personal disputes.

Justice of the peace courts are ruled by a local magistrate (law official) appointed to preserve the peace in the area. Justices of the peace hear minor cases, grant licenses, perform marriages, and address other concerns of local law. Alderman's courts are led by an elected official of the city council. These courts deal with misdemeanors (nonviolent crimes), traffic offenses, parking violations, and minor civil (not criminal) matters.

## Local Government

Delaware is divided into three counties. Each county is governed by a council plus an elected executive or an appointed administrator. To keep track of taxes and other financial matters, each county is divided into smaller areas called hundreds.

## National Representation

The citizens of Delaware send two senators and one representative to the U.S. Congress. During national presidential elections, the small state has three Electoral College votes, the lowest possible number. Six other states also have only three Electoral College votes: Alaska, Montana, North Dakota, South Dakota, Vermont, and Wyoming. (As of 2004, California has the largest number of Electoral College votes — fifty-five — followed by Texas with thirty-four.) States are given Electoral College votes based on the sizes of their populations.

| General Assembly | | | |
|---|---|---|---|
| House | Number of Members | Length of Term | Term Limits |
| Senate | 21 senators | 4 years | none |
| House of Representatives | 41 representatives | 2 years | none |

## Delaware Politics

Both Democrats and Republicans have enjoyed periods of popularity in Delaware. Since the mid-1930s, the state has struck a balance between the two major U.S. political parties. The most recent trend is toward the Democrats. In 1988, a Democratic senator from Delaware tried to win his party's nomination for the presidential election. Joseph R. Biden Jr. did not get the nomination, but he continues to be a respected Democrat in Congress.

As a large and powerful employer in the state, the du Pont family has influenced Delaware's politics for generations. Pierre Samuel du Pont IV sought the Republican nomination in that same 1988 presidential election. Du Pont served in Delaware's house of representatives for one term in 1968 and then served three terms in the U.S. Congress before he was elected governor of Delaware in 1976 and again in 1980. After a poor showing in the New Hampshire primary election, du Pont, like Biden, withdrew from the presidential race.

## Government for the People

One of the main functions of state government is to help local citizens. Delaware's Health and Social Services (DHSS) department is the fifth-largest employer in the state, providing work for more than one-third of all state employees. The department's mission is "To improve the quality of life for Delaware's citizens by promoting health and well-being, fostering self-sufficiency, and protecting vulnerable populations." To accomplish these goals, the DHSS has eleven divisions. Each department under DHSS provides services to help all of Delaware's citizens. In addition, the DHSS helps Delawareans help each other by providing opportunities for volunteerism.

### Ruth Ann Minner

In 1992, Ruth Ann Minner became Delaware's first female lieutenant governor. Eight years later, she made history again by becoming the state's first female governor. When Minner was thirty-two, her husband died, leaving her to support their three sons. She worked two jobs while earning her high school and college degrees. She rose from page for the Delaware house of representatives to state representative and state senator. Minner has been named Delaware's Mother of the Year and Woman of the Year and was inducted into the state's Women's Hall of Fame.

▶ One of the oldest towns in Delaware, New Castle was the capital of the Delaware Colony.

# Ballet and Baseball

> Variety's the very spice of life.
> —*William Cowper*
> *in his 1785 poem* "The Task"

Delaware's history since the first European settlement is displayed throughout the state. The Zwaanendael Museum in Lewes recalls the arrival of the Dutch in 1631. The museum is a replica of a Dutch town hall. Exhibits tell the story of Zwaanendael, that first ill-fated Dutch settlement; the 1798 wreck of *HM Brig DeBraak*, a Dutch ship; and the 1813 bombardment of Lewes by the British. Lewes has many preserved old buildings, including an 1850s doctor's office, a blacksmith shop, and a Swedish-style Plank House furnished as a settler's cabin. More evidence of Delaware's Swedish settlers can be found at Wilmington's Kalmar Nyckel Shipyard. This living-history shipyard and museum features an authentic re-creation of the tall ship that carried the first Swedish settlers to Delaware in 1638. Visitors also learn the history of shipbuilding in the state.

Evidence of Delaware's journey from colony to state can be seen in downtown Wilmington. Rodney Square honors the patriot whose vote helped the American colonies declare independence from England. At the center is a statue of Rodney on a horse. Visitors to Newark can see Cooch's Bridge, where the outnumbered troops of General George Washington rallied under the new Stars and Stripes flag.

▼ Some 12,500 Confederate prisoners escaped the horrible conditions of this Civil War prison on Pea Patch Island despite its strong walls and moat. The prison is now part of Fort Delaware State Park.

After the Revolution, the new nation had to shape its own government. One of the framers of the U.S. Constitution was John Dickinson, whose boyhood home can be visited near Dover. At the John Dickinson Plantation, guides in historic clothing show how "the Penman of the American Revolution" and his family, tenants, and slaves lived.

The town of New Castle offers many preserved historic buildings, including Amstel House, an eighteenth-century mansion where George Washington attended a wedding. Built in 1732, New Castle Court House served as the colony's capitol and then Delaware's first state capitol. George Read II House and Garden were built in 1801 by the son of one of the signers of the Declaration of Independence.

The 235-acre (95-ha) Hagley Museum and Library is located on the site of Eleuthère Irénée du Pont's first factory on the Brandywine River in Wilmington. The museum includes the family's first mansion, built by du Pont in 1803, plus artifacts from America's early industrial days, such as the first DuPont company office, the original gunpowder mills, an 1814 cotton mill, and a working 1870s machine shop.

Fort Delaware State Park contains Pea Patch Island, where the solid granite walls of a Civil War prison confined captured Confederate soldiers. Nature trails on the island give visitors a look at the nesting grounds of many birds.

## The Nanticokes

The Nanticokes of Sussex County are the only tribe that still calls Delaware home. Millsboro's Nanticoke Indian Museum resides in a former community schoolhouse that is now on the National Register of Historic Landmarks. The museum displays local pottery, spear points, arrowheads, and clothing. Its library contains Native American books and photographs. The museum also sells basketwork, beadwork, featherwork, pottery, and "dream catchers," ornaments that supposedly protect their owners from evil spirits in dreams while asleep.

Dover Air Force Base recalls Delaware's participation in World War II. The largest U.S. Air Force base in the East now houses the Air Mobility Command Museum, with exhibits tracing the history of U.S. air power, including a C-47A with D-Day invasion stripes and other planes.

No visit to Delaware would be complete without the timeless pleasure of a trip to the beach. Rehoboth Beach is the state's busiest resort. The busy beach town was originally developed in 1873 for religious summer camp meetings run by the Methodist Church. Rehoboth is a Biblical term that means "open spaces." Today, thanks to the century-old mansions on its leafy lanes, the resort combines the appeal of history with sandy beaches. Visitors seeking a simpler setting go to resorts such as Bethany Beach and Fenwick Island, near the Maryland border.

## Libraries and Museums

Delaware's cultural institutions are concentrated in the north. Wilmington is home to the state's excellent art museum, history museum, and museum of natural history. The Delaware Art Museum is best known for its collection

▲ The Johnson Victrola Museum honors Eldridge Reeves Johnson, founder of the Victrola Talking Machine Company. Visitors view talking machines, records, and other company memorabilia.

### DID YOU KNOW?

The Delaware Museum of Natural History's permanent collection includes a 500-pound (227-kilogram) clam! The museum also displays the bones of Delaware's only dinosaurs.

of American art, including works by Delaware native Howard Pyle and his student, Maxfield Parrish. Dioramas showing extinct birds and African animals in lifelike poses, an extensive shell collection, and a model of Australia's Great Barrier Reef are just some of the attractions at the Delaware Museum of Natural History. Wilmington also contains the state's two largest libraries: the research library of the Historical Society of Delaware and the Wilmington Public Library. Many fascinating smaller museums and galleries can be found throughout the state.

## Communications

Delaware has two daily newspapers and several weeklies. Wilmington's *News Journal* began publication in 1785, but it was then called the *Delaware Gazette*. The *Delaware State News* is published in Dover.

The state's newspapers, radio, and television are largely of local interest, but Delaware's public television reaches Philadelphia. Similarly, northern Delawareans can enjoy programming broadcast by Philadelphia's radio and television stations. Delaware's first radio station, WDEL in Wilmington, started broadcasting in 1922.

▼ The Riverfront Arts Center attracts visitors to its art exhibits, concerts, theater productions, and riverfront path.

## Music and Theater

For a small state, Delaware offers a great deal of entertainment. Wilmington has many theaters. The Grand Opera House serves as the Delaware Center for Performing Arts and frequently hosts OperaDelaware, the Delaware Symphony Orchestra, and famous performers from all over the world in its 1,190-seat Victorian theater. Its new neighbor, "Baby Grand," is a 300-seat theater where Delawareans can enjoy art films and chamber music. OperaDelaware, established in 1945, is the fourteenth-oldest opera company in the nation. The First USA Riverfront Arts Center has a 275-seat theater and a 25,000-square-foot (2,323-square-meter) main exhibition area. The center was built in an old World War II ship-assembly building on the Christina River. The Playhouse Theatre in Wilmington's historic Hotel du Pont is known as "Little Broadway" because it has hosted touring companies of Broadway shows for over eighty years. Lucille Ball, a famous comedian, is among the many great performers who have graced its stage. Wilmington also has several dinner theaters.

In addition to exhibits of visual arts, the Christina Cultural Arts Center presents music and dance performances designed to promote ethnic awareness, as does the University of Delaware Center for Black Culture in Newark. Wilmington's Caribbean Cultural Association also presents performances by locally based West Indian dance and music troupes.

Ballet Theatre of Dover puts on four shows each year. Professional guest dancers from the New York City Ballet, England's Royal Ballet, and Russia's Bolshoi Ballet have joined the company's student performers. The Delaware Ballet Company teams with OperaDelaware for shows at the Grand Opera

▲ Delaware's Grand Opera House presents performances of operas, ballets, and classical and popular music.

**DID YOU KNOW?**

**D**elaware hosts the nation's largest men's high school basketball invitational tournament. Over thirty teams representing twenty states come to Cape Henlopen High School for an event known as Slam Dunk to the Beach.

House and also presents performances at Delaware State University and smaller venues.

## Outdoor Fun

Delaware is too small to have its own major football, baseball, basketball, or hockey teams, but it does have a professional men's soccer team, the Delaware Wizards. The state offers many forms of outdoor fun: hiking, biking, horseback riding, bird-watching, swimming, boating, camping, fishing, hunting, and more. Delaware also has many excellent golf courses. Each spring, the DuPont Country Club hosts the McDonald's LPGA Championship, one of the four major annual events in women's golf.

The University of Delaware is home to one of the largest clubs belonging to the United States Figure Skating Association. Some world-class competitors have sharpened their skating skills at the university's figure skating club, including Tara Lipinski. The Fred Rust Ice Arena at the Newark campus features exciting events on ice.

Several famous racetracks are located in Delaware. Harrington Raceway is the nation's oldest continuously operating harness racing facility. Dover Downs and Wilmington's Delaware Park also offer harness racing.

▼ Opened in 1993, Judy Johnson Field at Frawley Stadium was named for Wilmington Negro League third baseman Judy Johnson, who was inducted into the National Baseball Hall of Fame, and Mayor Dan Frawley. Frawley, a great supporter of building the stadium, died in February 1993.

### Delaware Greats

**R**andy White, co-Most Valuable Player in football's Super Bowl XII, began his career at Thomas McKean High School in Wilmington. He went on to win the Lombardi Award while at the University of Maryland. As a pro football player, White failed to play only one game in fourteen seasons, making him one of the most durable players in the National Football League (NFL). Known as "the Manster" — half man, half monster — White was elected to the Pro Football Hall of Fame in 1994.

**F**rawley Stadium is the home of Wilmington's Blue Rocks baseball team. The Blue Rocks are a Carolina League Class A farm team of the Kansas City Royals. The team produced the American League's 1999 Rookie of the Year, Carlos Beltran. Other Blue Rocks who have made it to the major leagues are Johnny Damon and Mike Sweeney.

# Delaware's Diamonds

> My ultimate goal is to avoid needless death and promote well-being for the largest number of people by establishing a philosophy that will eliminate war.
>
> — *Dr. Henry Jay Heimlich, inventor of the Heimlich maneuver*

Following are a few of the thousands of people who were born, died, or spent much of their lives in Delaware and made extraordinary contributions to the state and the nation.

## CAESAR RODNEY
### POLITICIAN AND JUDGE

**BORN:** *October 7, 1728, Poplar Grove*
**DIED:** *June 29, 1784, Dover*

**B**y the time America's Second Continental Congress was meeting in Philadelphia from 1775 to 1776, Caesar Rodney had been a justice of the peace, a Delaware Supreme Court justice, a member of the Delaware Assembly, and a captain in a Delaware militia. Now he was one of the state's three delegates to the Continental Congress. Rodney's vote would decide whether or not Delaware would favor declaring independence from England. Rodney was at home, extremely ill, when he heard that the crucial vote would be taken in just a few days. Rodney jumped on his horse and rode 80 miles (129 km) through a rainstorm to cast his vote for independence. A statue in Wilmington shows Rodney on his horse.

## OLIVER EVANS
### INVENTOR

**BORN:** *September 13, 1755, Newport*
**DIED:** *April 15, 1819, New York, NY*

**A**s a young man working in a flour mill, Oliver Evans invented a water-powered mill in which grain was moved automatically through the various processes by a series of conveyors. This fully automated mill, which took just one person to run, became a prototype for future factories. Evans also built one of the first high-pressure steam engines, which vastly improved the milling process, formerly powered by waterwheels. Evans's "amphibious digger," a steam-powered dredge used to clear mud from riverbeds or harbors, is considered America's first self-propelled land vehicle. Between 1807 and 1817, Evans built more than one hundred steam engines. He proposed numerous technical advances, including artificial refrigeration that used a steam pump to make ether evaporate quickly.

# ELEUTHÈRE IRÉNÉE DU PONT
## BUSINESS LEADER

**BORN:** *June 24, 1771, Paris, France*
**DIED:** *October 31, 1834, Philadelphia, PA*

**B**orn into a wealthy family in Paris, Eleuthère Irénée du Pont was seventeen when he began studying under scientist Antoine Lavoisier at the French gunpowder works. He was twenty-eight when he brought his family to the United States to escape the dangers of the French Revolution (1789–1799) and the violence that followed it. In 1802, du Pont founded a gunpowder mill on the banks of the Brandywine River near Wilmington. The DuPont corporation eventually grew into one of the nations most successful business empires.

# RICHARD ALLEN
## RELIGIOUS LEADER

**BORN:** *February 14, 1760, Philadelphia, PA*
**DIED:** *March 26, 1831, Philadelphia, PA*

**B**orn a slave in Philadelphia, Richard Allen grew up on a Delaware plantation. After buying his freedom, Allen became a Methodist minister. He preached occasionally at St. George's Methodist Episcopal Church in Philadelphia. When whites at St. George's forced blacks to leave during one of his sermons, Allen and the rejected churchgoers organized the Free African Society. In 1793, this society became Bethel Church, an independent Methodist church. In 1799, Allen became the first African American to be appointed a deacon of the Methodist Church. In 1816, representatives from several African-American Methodist churches organized the African Methodist Episcopal Church as the nation's first black denomination. Allen was chosen to be their bishop. During his ministry, Allen involved the church in various causes, including the antislavery movement.

# HOWARD PYLE
## ILLUSTRATOR

**BORN:** *March 5, 1853, Wilmington*
**DIED:** *November 9, 1911, Florence, Italy*

**H**oward Pyle spent almost his entire life in Delaware. Pyle traveled to art school in Philadelphia and New York city. His imaginative, colorful paintings quickly earned him work at top magazines such as *Harper's Weekly*. Pyle's passion for historical detail gave special life to his illustrations for classic books such as *The Merry Adventures of Robin Hood*. During his thirty-five-year career, Pyle wrote and illustrated nineteen books for children and produced some thirty-three hundred published illustrations. In his later years, Pyle devoted himself to teaching. He helped develop the talents of artists such as Maxfield Parrish and N. C. Wyeth. In 1900, he founded the Howard Pyle School of Art in Wilmington, which offered free classes in illustration.

# ANNIE JUMP CANNON
## ASTRONOMER

**BORN:** *December 11, 1863, Dover*
**DIED:** *April 13, 1941, Cambridge, MA*

**A**t sixteen, Annie Jump Cannon became one of Delaware's first women to go to college. After graduating from Wellesley College in Massachusetts, she joined the staff of the Harvard College Observatory. There she helped develop the Harvard classification system of spectra, a way of classifying stars. Cannon became known as "the Census Taker of the Sky" because of her many years discovering and describing stars, classifying an average of 5,000 stars a month. In her lifetime, she catalogued about 350,000 stars and similar heavenly bodies. Cannon pioneered the classification of stars by color. She was also the first woman to whom England's famous Oxford University gave an honorary doctorate. She started an American Astronomical Society prize honoring female astronomers.

# WILLIAM JULIUS "JUDY" JOHNSON
## BASEBALL PLAYER

**BORN:** *October 26, 1889, Snow Hill, MD*
**DIED:** *June 15, 1989, Wilmington*

**W**illiam Julius Johnson was a star third baseman in the Negro Leagues and one of the greatest third basemen of all time. African Americans were not allowed to play major league baseball until 1947, so they played in the Negro Leagues. Johnson played in the Negro Leagues from 1918 to 1937, for the Philadelphia Hilldales, Homestead Grays, and Pittsburgh Crawfords. He was valued as a positive influence on other players for his grace under pressure and his intelligent approach to baseball. Johnson led the Hilldales to three pennants from 1923 to 1925, with batting averages of over .390 all three years. After he retired from baseball, Johnson drove a cab in Wilmington until he was hired as a scout for the Atlanta Braves and the Philadelphia Phillies. As a scout, Johnson brought many young African-American players to the major leagues. In 1975, Johnson was inducted into the National Baseball Hall of Fame. Judy Johnson Field in Wilmington is named after him.

# WALLACE HUME CAROTHERS
## CHEMIST

**BORN:** *April 27, 1896, Burlington, IA*
**DIED:** *April 29, 1937, Philadelphia, PA*

As a child, Wallace Carothers was fascinated by tools and mechanical devices. He was so good at chemistry that Missouri's Tarkio College made him a chemistry instructor before he even graduated. After earning his Ph.D. in organic chemistry in 1924, Carothers taught chemistry at Harvard. Because of his reputation as a brilliant researcher, DuPont hired him in 1928 to lead its new research program. Carothers developed nylon, the world's first synthetic fiber, which quickly became as familiar as wool, silk, wood, or steel, the natural materials it often replaces. He also developed the first synthetic rubber, neoprene. Carothers was the first industrial chemist to be elected to the National Academy of Sciences. He loved classical music and was an avid reader of poetry.

# HENRY JAY HEIMLICH
## DOCTOR

**BORN:** *February 20, 1920, Wilmington*

Henry Jay Heimlich graduated from Cornell Medical School and then worked as both a doctor and a professor in New York and later Cincinnati. His major field of study was disorders of the alimentary tract (the path of food through the body). Heimlich gained fame for developing the "Heimlich maneuver," a way to save someone who is choking. Through the 1960s, choking was a leading cause of accidental death in the United States. Heimlich realized that squeezing a person would force air out of the lungs, often expelling the object causing the choking. After Heimlich published a study on the maneuver in 1974, it started saving lives and became well known. Since then, the number of choking deaths has dropped dramatically. He is now the president of the Heimlich Institute.

# GEORGE THOROGOOD
## MUSICIAN

**BORN:** *February 24, 1950, Wilmington*

George Thorogood was not interested in music as a child. Then at twenty, he was inspired to start making music after seeing a concert by blues legend John Lee Hooker. Thorogood and his band, the Destroyers, first performed at Lane Hall at the University of Delaware on December 1, 1973. The band gained experience playing small clubs in Boston. In 1977, they released their first album. The next album, *Move It On Over,* gained national radio attention. The Destroyers have released over a dozen albums and performed with legends such as Bo Diddley, ZZ Top, and the Rolling Stones. Thorogood is so identified with his home state that some fans call his band the Delaware Destroyers. They are known for exciting live shows and a solid combination of rock and roll with blues. Their popular song "Bad to the Bone" was used in the movie *Christine,* based on the Stephen King novel. Thorogood has also been a semiprofessional baseball player.

# Delaware

## History At-A-Glance

**Ancient Times**
The Lenni Lenape and Nanticoke tribes live in present-day Delaware.

**1631**
Dutch found Delaware's first European settlement in Swan Valley. Zwaanendael is destroyed by 1632.

**1664**
British take possession of New Netherland (renamed New York). The land they take includes Delaware.

**1701**
Delaware, now known as Three Lower Counties of Pennsylvania, asks for its own legislature.

**1743**
Newark College, later the University of Delaware, opens.

**1776**
Caesar Rodney rides to Philadelphia to break tie vote and ratify Declaration of Independence.

**1609**
Henry Hudson, an Englishman sailing for the Dutch, enters Delaware Bay and becomes first European to see the area.

**1638**
Swedish colonists found Delaware's first permanent European settlement, Fort Christina, near Wilmington.

**1682**
Delaware is given to Pennsylvania's founder, William Penn.

**1704**
Delaware's first independent legislature meets.

**1754**
Delaware's first library opens in Wilmington.

**1777**
Americans retreat at Battle of Cooch's Bridge, near Newark. Dover becomes capital of Delaware.

| 1600 | 1700 | 1800 |
|------|------|------|

**1492**
Christopher Columbus comes to New World.

**1607**
Capt. John Smith and three ships land on Virginia coast and start first English settlement in New World — Jamestown.

**1754–63**
French and Indian War.

**1773**
Boston Tea Party.

**1776**
Declaration of Independence adopted July 4.

**1777**
Articles of Confederation adopted by Continental Congress.

**1787**
U.S. Constitution written.

**1812–14**
War of 1812.

# United States

## History At-A-Glance

**1785**
The *Delaware Gazette* becomes Delaware's first successful newspaper. Oliver Evans improves flour milling machinery.

**1787**
Delaware casts first vote in favor of U.S. Constitution and becomes the first state.

**1802**
The du Pont empire begins when Eleuthère Irénée du Pont establishes a powder mill on the banks of the Brandywine River.

**1829**
Chesapeake and Delaware Canal opens, connecting Chesapeake Bay and Delaware River. Delaware establishes a public school system.

**1861–65**
Delaware fights for the Union during Civil War, despite many Delawareans' sympathy for the South.

**1897**
Delaware adopts its fourth and current constitution.

**1917–18**
Ten thousand Delawareans fight in World War I.

**1938**
The DuPont Corporation introduces nylon to the public.

**1951**
The Delaware Memorial Bridge spans the Delaware River, connecting Delaware and New Jersey.

**1971**
State legislature passes the Coastal Zone Act, banning the building of industrial plants on the coastline.

**1981**
Delaware enacts the Financial Center Development Act, encouraging out-of-state banks to open corporate offices in Delaware.

**1987**
Delaware's 200th birthday.

**1800**  **1900**  **2000**

**1848**
Gold discovered in California draws eighty thousand prospectors in the 1849 Gold Rush.

**1861–65**
Civil War.

**1869**
Transcontinental railroad completed.

**1917–18**
U.S. involvement in World War I.

**1929**
Stock market crash ushers in Great Depression.

**1941–45**
U.S. involvement in World War II.

**1950–53**
U.S. fights in the Korean War.

**1964–73**
U.S. involvement in Vietnam War.

**2000**
George W. Bush wins the closest presidential election in history.

**2001**
A terrorist attack in which four hijacked airliners crash into New York City's World Trade Center, the Pentagon, and farmland in western Pennsylvania leaves thousands dead or injured.

◀ **The lighthouse on Cape Henlopen, Delaware Bay, as it appeared in 1780.**

# Festivals and Fun for All

Check web site for exact date and directions.

### Brandywine Zoo, Wilmington

Delaware's only zoo features wild and exotic animals from North and South America and temperate Asia. Programs for children take place throughout the year. www.k12.de.us/warner/zoointro.htm

### Caribbean Festival, Wilmington

This colorful Caribbean cultural experience includes children's activities, costumes, music, dancing, food, arts, crafts, and more. http://www.cariculture-de.org/festival.html

### Delaware Agricultural Museum and Village, Dover

The museum's Loockerman Landing Village shows a rural community of the 1890s with a one-room schoolhouse, a barbershop, a store, and a train station. In December, visitors celebrate A Farmer's Christmas. www.agriculturalmuseum.org

### Delaware State News Sandcastle Contests, Rehoboth Beach

Both children and adults compete by building fantastic sand sculptures. www.sandcastlecentral.com/contests/bymonth/aug.html

### Delaware State Fair, Harrington

For ten days beginning on the third Thursday in July, visitors enjoy concerts, demolition derbies, carnival rides, and view hundreds of animals and thousands of exhibits. www.delawarestatefair.com

### Delmarva Folk Festival, Hartly

For over a decade, Delaware Friends of Folk have presented this popular folk music festival, formerly called the Fall Fling. www.delfolk.org

### DuPont RiverFest, Wilmington

This annual festival at Tubman-Garrett Riverfront Park and the Port of Wilmington features water rides, crafts, contests, demonstrations, and live music. www.dupontriverfest.com

### Johnson Victrola Museum, Dover

This museum features inventions and personal items relating to Eldridge Reeves Johnson, who was the founder of an early brand of record players. Exhibits include a 1920s Victrola dealer's store with talking machines, Victrolas, early records, and information about popular recording artists. www.dcet.k12.de.us/wayne/museum/victrola.html

### Lums Pond State Park, south of Newark

Built around the state's largest freshwater pond, the park offers fishing, camping, and boat rentals. A "sensory trail" encourages visitors to use all their senses, not just sight. Other trails are for biking, hiking, horseback riding, and snowmobiling.
www.destateparks.com

### Nanticoke Indian Powwow, east of Millsboro

This annual September celebration features singing, dancing, storytelling, drumming, Native American foods, and crafts.
www.millsboro.org/nanticokemuseum.asp

### New Castle Court House Museum, New Castle

Built on the site of Delaware's first courthouse of 1689, the New Castle Court House is now a museum where visitors learn about Delaware's history, colonial law, and the Underground Railroad.
www.destatemuseums.org/ncch/museum.html

### Oktoberfest, Newark

Each year on the third weekend in September, visitors enjoy brass bands, dancing, German food, and amusement rides.
www.delawaresaengerbund.org

### Rehoboth Beach Chocolate Festival, Rehoboth and Dewey Beaches

Chocolate lovers gather for dessert-baking contests and get to sample the winning entries.
http://www.rehomain.com/calendar

### Sea Witch Halloween & Fiddlers Festival, Rehoboth and Dewey Beaches

For two days at the end of October, families enjoy a bonfire on the beach, a costume parade and contest, a classic car show, a sea witch hunt, a golf tournament, a best pet-costume contest, and more.
www.beach-fun.com

### World Championship Punkin Chunkin' Competition, Millsboro

Since 1986, contestants have competed to see who can throw a pumpkin the farthest by human power or catapult. Tailgate picnics and bands add to the squishy fun.
www.worldchampionshippunkinchunkin.com/

▶ More than 5,000 people assemble in an empty field at Millsboro every year to watch pumpkins fly.

## Books

Hesse, Karen. *A Light in the Storm: The Civil War Diary of Amelia Martin, Fenwick Island, Delaware, 1861*. New York: Scholastic, 1999. Part of the *Dear America* series of historical fiction, this book describes the life of a lighthouse keeper's daughter whose family is being torn apart by the Civil War.

Keehn, Sally M. *Moon of Two Dark Horses*. New York: Philomel Books, 1995. A historical novel concerning the friendship between a young Delaware brave and a settler's son during the Revolutionary War.

Laird, Marnie. *Water Rat*. Delray Beach, FL: Winslow Press, 1998. Set in 1748, this historical novel tells the story of a fourteen-year-old orphan with disabilities who triumphs over the pirates who plagued Delaware's waters.

Marsh, Carole. *Delaware Silly Trivia!* Peachtree City, GA: Gallopade, 1990. Fun facts about the state's history, geography, and more.

Wilker, Joshua D. G. *The Lenape Indians (Junior Library of American Indians)*. Broomall, PA: Chelsea House, 1994. Details the life of Delaware's Native Americans.

## Web Sites

▶ Official state web site
www.state.de.us

▶ Tourism
www.visitdelaware.com

▶ Historical Society
www.hsd.org

▶ Museums
www.destatemuseums.org

▶ Native Americans
www.delawaretribeofindians.nsn.us

Note: Page numbers in *italics* refer to maps, illustrations, or photographs.